STARGAZERS

GAIL GIBBONS

Holiday House • New York

STARGAZERS

For Lance Osadchey

Special thanks to Professor Edward Foley,
teacher of astronomy, St. Michael's College,
Colchester, Vermont.

Library of Congress Cataloging-in-Publication Data
Gibbons, Gail.
    Stargazers / by Gail Gibbons.
        p.   cm.
    Summary: Tells what stars are, why they twinkle, how
constellations were named, how telescopes are used to
study stars, and more.
    ISBN 0-8234-0983-X   ISBN 0-8234-1507-4 (pbk.)
    1. Astronomy—Juvenile literature.   2. Astronomy—Observers'
manuals—Juvenile literature.   3. Stars—Observers' manuals—
Juvenile literature.   [1. Astronomy.   2. Stars.]   I. Title.
QB46.G42   1992   92-52713   CIP   AC
520—dc20

Not long after the sun sets, the sky becomes darker and darker. On clear nights points of light begin to appear in the sky.

These points of light are stars. Stars give off heat and light because of their hot gases, which make stars shine.

Stargazers are people who watch the night sky. Some stargazers are called astronomers. Astronomers know a lot about stars.

Some stars are bigger, some are smaller. Most stars are very large. The sun is a yellow star. It is over a million times larger than our planet Earth. All the other stars in the night sky look tiny because they are so much farther away.

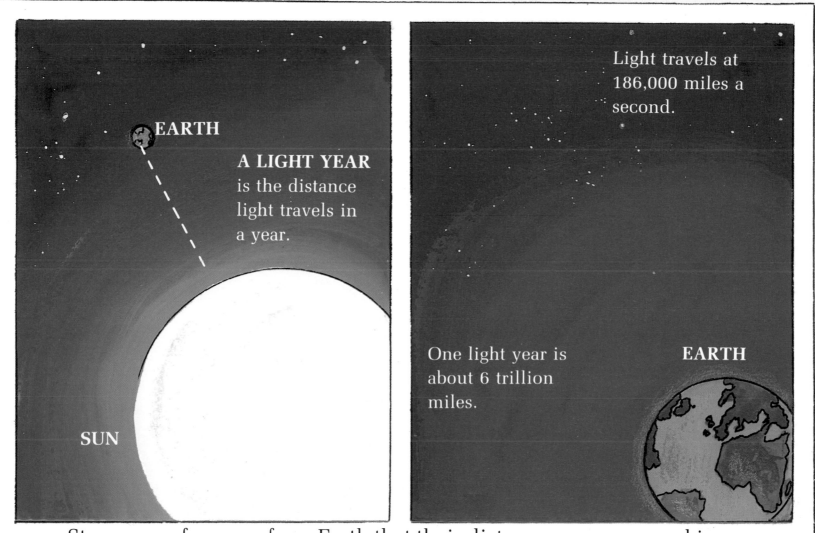

EARTH

A LIGHT YEAR is the distance light travels in a year.

SUN

Light travels at 186,000 miles a second.

One light year is about 6 trillion miles.

EARTH

Stars are so far away from Earth that their distances are measured in light years, not miles. The sun is eight light minutes from us. The next star is four light years away. Some stars are billions of light years away!

Some stars look brighter than others. Also stars are different colors. Some look red, some are yellow and others look white. The cooler stars are red, the warmer stars are yellow and the hotter stars are bluish white.

Stars look like they twinkle, too. This is because of the air around Earth, called the atmosphere. As starlight travels through the atmosphere, it makes some stars look like they are twinkling.

During the night, the stars move across the sky from east to west. This is because the planet Earth turns slowly from west to east. The stars rise and set just like the sun does.

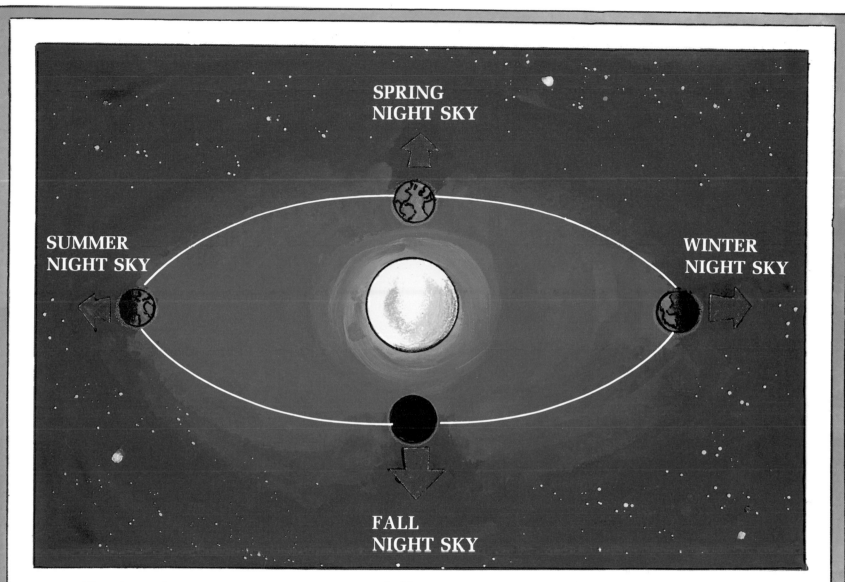

During the year, stargazers see different stars in the night. There are stars in the sky during the day, too. They can't be seen because of the bright sunlight.

MILKY WAY

The **MILKY WAY**
is a **GALAXY**.

The Milky Way seems milky because it looks like a white, cloudy band across the sky.

A **GALAXY** is made up of many billions of stars. Our planet Earth is part of the Milky Way galaxy.

It is made up of separate stars, too many to count! They blend together because they are very dim and are very, very far away.

A CONSTELLATION is a group of bright stars.

Long ago, people thought that certain groups of bright stars formed outlines of people, animals or things in the sky. They gave them names. These star groups are called constellations. Some of the names sound strange. They came down from the Romans who spoke Latin. Today's stargazers and astronomers still use these old names.

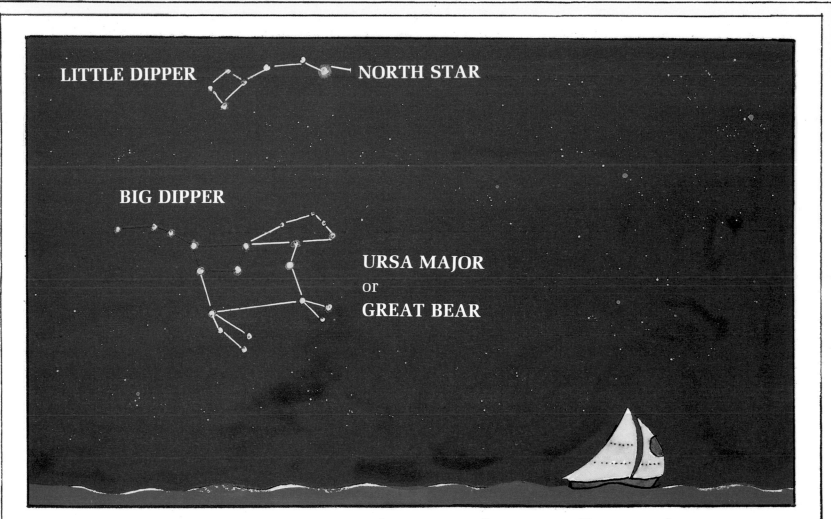

The Big Dipper is a pattern of stars in the constellation of Ursa Major, or the Great Bear. Nearby is the Little Dipper. The star at the end of the Little Dipper's handle is the North Star. The North Star has been used to guide people on their journeys for hundreds of years.

One constellation was named Orion, after a famous hunter, and is seen in the winter in the southern night sky. Long ago, people thought the star group looked like a hunter with a club, shield, and belt.

THE GREATER DOG has
the brightest star
in the night sky.
It is called **SIRIUS,**
the Dog Star.

CANIS MAJOR
or
GREATER DOG

Near Orion is a group of stars that people thought looked like a dog.
It is called the constellation of Canis Major or the Greater Dog.

There are 88 constellations. Some of them are seen at different times of the year.

STAR CHART

STAR CHART

Stargazers and astronomers can locate the stars and constellations in the sky by looking at star charts. Star charts are maps of the sky. Sometimes it may take time and patience to find a special star or constellation.

About 2000 stars can be seen while looking up at the sky on a clear, dark night. Some stargazers use a pair of binoculars to get a better look at a star or a small group of stars.

Other stargazers and astronomers gaze through telescopes. They are able to see some stars clearer, and also other stars that are too far away to be seen with eyes alone.

REFRACTING TELESCOPE

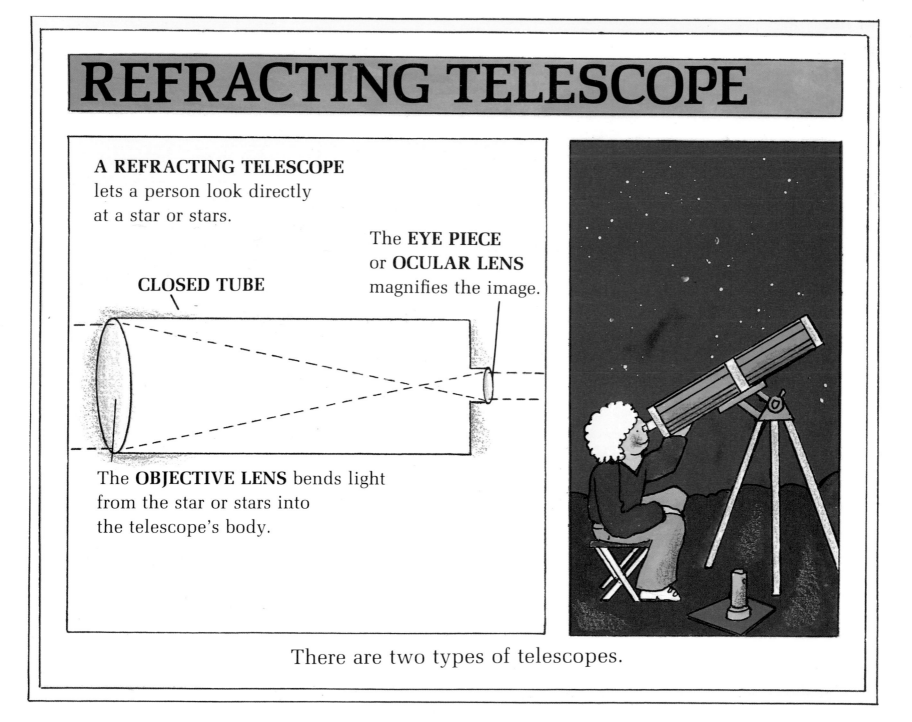

A REFRACTING TELESCOPE
lets a person look directly
at a star or stars.

The **EYE PIECE**
or **OCULAR LENS**
magnifies the image.

CLOSED TUBE

The **OBJECTIVE LENS** bends light
from the star or stars into
the telescope's body.

There are two types of telescopes.

REFLECTING TELESCOPE

A REFLECTING TELESCOPE
lets a person look at a reflection of a
star or stars by using two mirrors.

CLOSED TUBE

The **FLAT MIRROR** reflects
the image to the **EYE PIECE.**

The **MAGNIFYING EYE PIECE**
picks up the image from the
flat mirror and makes it larger.

The **CONCAVE MIRROR** collects
and reflects the light from
the star or stars back up
the telescope's body.

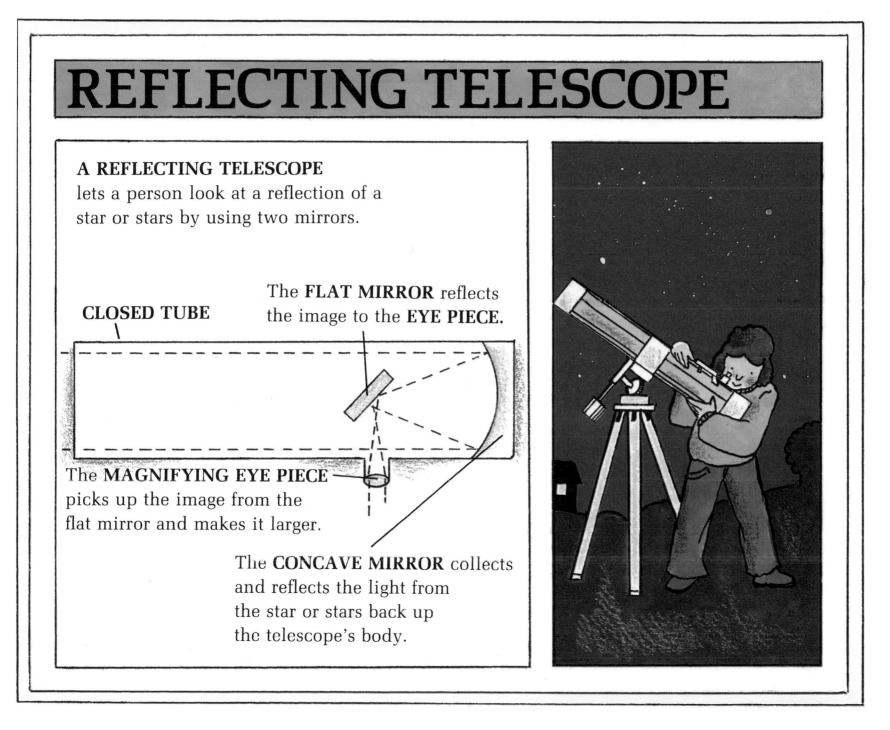

OBSERVATORY

Some telescopes are huge. They are in observatories where astronomers study the skies.

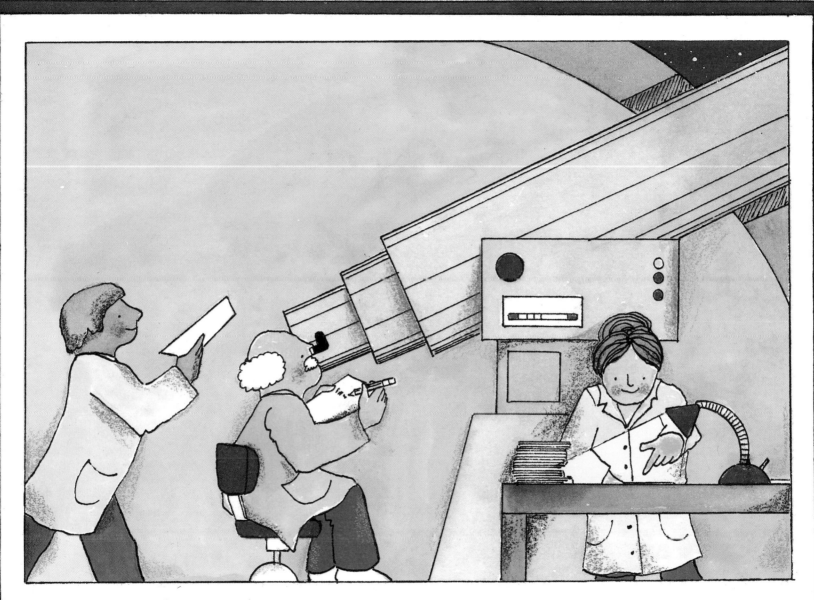

Most telescopes can take pictures that the astronomers can study later. They are always making new discoveries.

People can go to planetariums to find out about stars. They sit in a circular room. The lights dim and everyone looks up.

A special machine shows the motions of the stars and planets on the domed ceiling. What a beautiful sight! The planetarium director explains what and where the different stars, constellations, and planets are.

At night the sky sparkles with thousands of stars. The more you study the stars and constellations the more you will learn. It's fun to be a stargazer!

Stargazing History

EARLY TIMES Some people thought certain stars were gods. If they saw a shooting star, they thought the gods were angry.

1608 The first telescope was invented by a Dutch eye doctor named Hans Lippershey. It was a refracting telescope.

1609 The Italian astronomer, Galileo, was the first to use a telescope to study the night skies.

1668 Issac Newton built the first reflecting telescope.

1840 For the first time photographs were taken through a telescope.

1937 The first radio telescope was invented. A radio telescope picks up radio waves and makes pictures from them.

1970 The biggest telescope in the world is in Arecibo, Puerto Rico. It is a radio telescope.

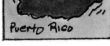

TODAY Some satellites carry telescopes. They send pictures back to Earth for astronomers to study.

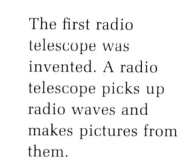

...Stars...Stars...Stars...Stars...Stars...

A shooting star isn't a star. It is a flash of light caused by a meteoroid burning up as it passes through Earth's atmosphere.

An average galaxy contains about 100,000 million stars.

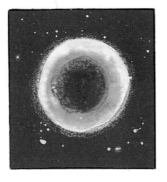

The center of a star is very hot. It can reach a temperature of 29 million degrees Fahrenheit (16 million degrees Centigrade).

About every 18 days our galaxy gives birth to a new star.

Sometimes when a star dies, it makes an explosion. The explosion is brighter than 1000 million suns!

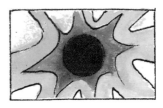

A neutron star is a star that is dying. It is very dense. One teaspoonful might weigh 40 million tons!

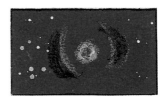

Sometimes, when a giant star dies, its gravity is so strong that it drags everything, including light, back to the star. The star becomes what is called a black hole.